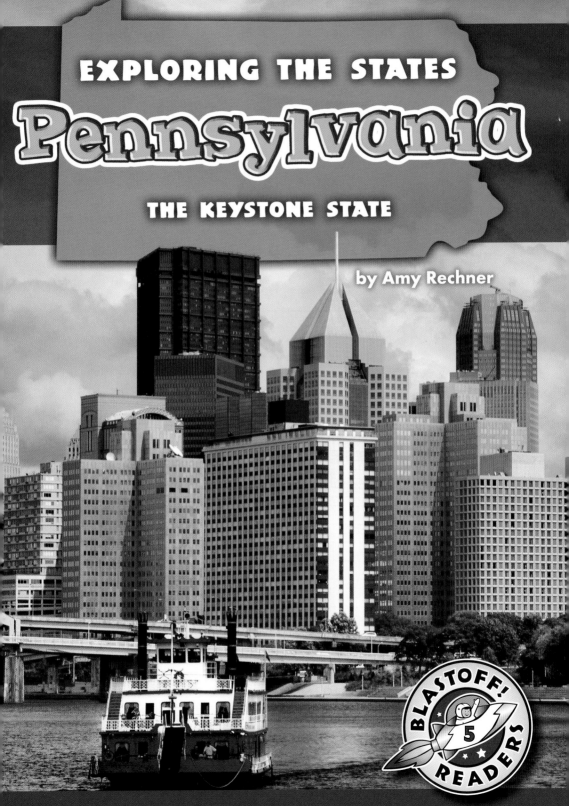

EXPLORING THE STATES

Pennsylvania

THE KEYSTONE STATE

by Amy Rechner

BLASTOFF! READERS 5

BELLWETHER MEDIA • MINNEAPOLIS, MN

Note to Librarians, Teachers, and Parents:

Blastoff! Readers are carefully developed by literacy experts and combine standards-based content with developmentally appropriate text.

Level 1 provides the most support through repetition of high-frequency words, light text, predictable sentence patterns, and strong visual support.

Level 2 offers early readers a bit more challenge through varied simple sentences, increased text load, and less repetition of high-frequency words.

Level 3 advances early-fluent readers toward fluency through increased text and concept load, less reliance on visuals, longer sentences, and more literary language.

Level 4 builds reading stamina by providing more text per page, increased use of punctuation, greater variation in sentence patterns, and increasingly challenging vocabulary.

Level 5 encourages children to move from "learning to read" to "reading to learn" by providing even more text, varied writing styles, and less familiar topics.

Whichever book is right for your reader, Blastoff! Readers are the perfect books to build confidence and encourage a love of reading that will last a lifetime!

This edition first published in 2014 by Bellwether Media, Inc.

No part of this publication may be reproduced in whole or in part without written permission of the publisher. For information regarding permission, write to Bellwether Media, Inc., Attention: Permissions Department, 5357 Penn Avenue South, Minneapolis, MN 55419.

Library of Congress Cataloging-in-Publication Data

Rechner, Amy.
 Pennsylvania / by Amy Rechner.
   pages cm. – (Blastoff! readers. Exploring the states)
 Includes bibliographical references and index.
 Summary: "Developed by literacy experts for students in grades three through seven, this book introduces young readers to the geography and culture of Pennsylvania"–Provided by publisher.
 ISBN 978-1-62617-037-7 (hardcover : alk. paper)
 1. Pennsylvania–Juvenile literature. I. Title.
 F149.3.R44 2014
 974.8–dc23

2013007783

Printed in the United States of America, North Mankato, MN.

Table of Contents

Where Is Pennsylvania?

Lake Erie

N
W E
S

Ohio

Pittsburgh

West Virginia

Pennsylvania is a rectangular state in the eastern United States. It touches six other states and one of the **Great Lakes**. The Delaware River forms its ragged eastern border. The capital city of Harrisburg is in the southeast.

New York

Delaware River

Pine Creek Gorge

Pennsylvania

New Jersey

Allentown •

Harrisburg ★

Philadelphia •

Maryland ← Delaware

Lake Erie curves along Pennsylvania's northwest corner. New York is to the north and wraps around the northeast corner. New Jersey meets Pennsylvania to the east. Delaware and Maryland lie to the south. West Virginia is southwest of Pennsylvania. Ohio shares the western border.

History

Native tribes lived in what is now Pennsylvania for thousands of years. Explorers came from Europe in the 1600s. In 1682, William Penn founded the **colony** of Pennsylvania. He was a **Quaker**. He believed people should be free to practice their faith. During the **Revolutionary War**, Philadelphia was the nation's capital city.

Battle of Gettysburg

Pennsylvania Timeline!

1608: John Smith of England travels up the Susquehanna River into what is now Pennsylvania.

1664: England takes control of the region from Dutch and Swedish settlers.

1681: King Charles II of England gives William Penn permission to set up the colony of Pennsylvania.

1763: Britain takes over western Pennsylvania after the French and Indian War.

1776: The Declaration of Independence is signed in Philadelphia.

1787: Pennsylvania becomes the second state.

1863: The Battle of Gettysburg is fought in southern Pennsylvania. It is one of the bloodiest battles of the Civil War.

1889: The city of Johnstown is destroyed in a flood after a dam breaks.

2001: On September 11, United Airlines flight 93 crashes near Shanksville. Passengers stop terrorists from crashing the plane in Washington, D.C.

Johnstown flood

Declaration signing

William Penn

The Land

Mountains and valleys cover much of Pennsylvania. The Appalachian Mountains cross the state from the northeast to the southwest. Mount Davis is the state's highest point at 3,213 feet (979 meters). The land in Pennsylvania's southeastern corner is more level. The **fertile** soil there is perfect for farming.

Allegheny Mountains

Pennsylvania's Climate
average °F

spring
Low: 40°
High: 60°

summer
Low: 62°
High: 82°

fall
Low: 45°
High: 63°

winter
Low: 24°
High: 39°

Many large rivers flow through Pennsylvania. Some of them provide passage through the mountains. The rivers and Lake Erie are important waterways for shipping. Pennsylvania's summers are hot. In winter, the north receives much more snow than the south.

Pine Creek Gorge

Pine Creek **Gorge** in the Tioga State Forest is known as Pennsylvania's Grand Canyon. Its towering sandstone cliffs were formed over the past 350 million years by the waters of Pine Creek. Now the gorge is nearly 47 miles (76 kilometers) long and up to 1,450 feet (442 meters) deep.

Unlike Arizona's Grand Canyon, Pine Creek Gorge features a lot of water. Waterfalls drop down **bluffs** into quiet pools. Pine Creek still flows through the gorge bottom. Hikers in Leonard Harrison State Park enjoy the gorge's beautiful scenery, especially in fall.

fun fact

Pine Creek Rail Trail runs along the bottom of the gorge. The trail used to be an old railroad bed. Now hikers, bikers, and horseback riders enjoy the tree-lined path.

heron

Pennsylvania's forests and mountains are home to many kinds of wildlife. White-tailed deer are seen all over the state. Elk and black bears roam the mountains in the north. Squirrels, rabbits, and raccoons scurry through woods and gardens. Turtles and snakes blend into the landscape.

white-tailed
deer

milkweed

groundhog

The woodlands are filled with maple, birch, oak, and fir trees. Falcons and owls perch on branches in search of prey. Wild turkeys and ruffed grouse stroll through fields and woods. Wildflowers such as milkweed and bee balm attract bees and fireflies. Ducks, geese, and herons fish along rivers filled with trout and pike.

Landmarks

Pennsylvania is home to more than 1,000 museums. In Harrisburg, the National **Civil War** Museum tells the story of the war from both sides. Nearby, Gettysburg National Military Park is a preserved Civil War battlefield.

The Carnegie Museums of Pittsburgh house exhibits in art, science, and natural history. Lancaster County offers a window into a different way of life. It is home to the **Pennsylvania Dutch**. People in this community choose to live simply. They avoid using modern inventions such as cars and telephones.

Carnegie Museum of Natural History

In Pittsburgh, visitors can ride "inclines" from downtown up to hilltop neighborhoods. Inclines are cable cars that travel along the side of a hill.

Philadelphia

Did you know?
From 1790 to 1800, Philadelphia served as the nation's capital while Washington, D.C. was being built.

Philadelphia is a modern city that shares space with 300 years of American history. The Comcast Center is Pennsylvania's tallest building. It rises only a few blocks from cobblestone streets and **colonial** houses. The cracked Liberty Bell is on display near Independence Hall. Visitors can see where the Declaration of Independence was signed. Nearby is the house where Betsy Ross sewed the first American flag.

Philadelphia attracts workers and students from around the world. It is easy to see this **diversity** at Reading Terminal Market. Its shops and stands feature **ethnic** foods of all kinds.

fun fact

The Liberty Bell rang in 1776 to announce independence from England. Seventy years later, a giant crack split the bell after it sounded in honor of George Washington's birthday.

Working

Did you know?

Crayola crayons and markers are made in Easton, Pennsylvania. Visitors can see how crayons are made and even take some home.

Pennsylvania's rich deposits of coal, iron ore, and oil fueled American progress. Pittsburgh was a center of steel and coal production in the 1800s and 1900s. Today, many Pennsylvanians work in **oil refineries**. Factory workers make machinery, metals, and food products.

One-fourth of Pennsylvania's land is used for farming. Farmers raise cattle, mushrooms, and Christmas trees. Most of Pennsylvania's workers have **service jobs**. They work in schools, hospitals, banks, and offices.

Where People Work in Pennsylvania

manufacturing
9%

services
78%

farming and
natural resources
2%

government
11%

Playing

Pennsylvania has something for everyone. **Scenic** hiking trails snake through mountains and valleys. Long days are spent fishing, boating, hunting, and horseback riding. Fly fishers are drawn to the state's many trout streams. Whitewater rafters and kayakers head to the Pocono Mountains for thrilling rides down the Lehigh River. In winter, the mountains attract downhill skiers.

Sports fans cheer for Pittsburgh or Philadelphia's professional teams. Little League baseball is also popular in Pennsylvania. The Little League World Series takes place in Williamsport. This city is home to the Little League Museum.

fun fact

Hersheypark is a big amusement park with shows, water rides, and roller coasters. It may be the only park in the country where visitors will see a Hershey's Kiss walk by!

Little League World Series

Shoofly Pie

Ingredients:

Unbaked pie crust

Crumbs: (Save 1/2 cup for topping)

2/3 cup brown sugar

1 tablespoon shortening

1 cup flour

Filling:

1 cup thick molasses

3/4 cup boiling water

1 egg, beaten

1 teaspoon baking soda

Directions:

1. Preheat oven to 375°F.

2. Bring water to a boil. Pour boiled water into a mixing bowl. Stir in baking soda. Then add the egg and molasses to the filling.

3. In a separate bowl, mix together brown sugar, shortening, and flour. Set aside 1/2 cup crumb mixture for the topping. Stir the rest of the mixture into the filling.

4. Pour the filling into the unbaked pie crust. Sprinkle 1/2 cup crumb mixture on top.

5. Bake for 10 minutes. Then reduce heat to 350°F. Bake until firm, about 35 to 45 minutes.

Note: The bottom may be wet when cut into, which is okay.

ice cream

! **fun fact**

Philadelphia-style ice cream is made without eggs. It is known across the country for its pure, rich flavor.

Wonderful food is found throughout Pennsylvania. Philadelphia is famous for the Philly cheesesteak sandwich. A soft roll is filled with thinly sliced beef and melted cheese for this classic meal. The state is also known for both hard and soft pretzels. Many restaurants slice the soft ones in half to make sandwiches.

The Pennsylvania Dutch are known for their many tasty foods, such as chicken pot pie and gooey shoofly pie. One unusual dish is scrapple. Pork and cornmeal are combined into a loaf that is sliced and fried. Want something sweet? Pennsylvania is home to both Marshmallow Peeps and Hershey's chocolate.

Festivals

Pennsylvanians enjoy year-round fun. The **Mummers** Parade in Philadelphia kicks off a wild celebration on New Year's Day. In February, the town of Ridgway hosts a chainsaw carving festival. More than 200 artists from around the world come to carve wood and ice sculptures.

Johnstown is known for the flood that destroyed the town in 1889. The city honors flood victims each May. Then it quickly cheers up with an annual **polka** festival. Gettysburg's Civil War Heritage Days attract thousands of people each June. Actors dress as soldiers and **reenact** the famous battle.

fun fact

The Kutztown Folk Festival celebrates the Pennsylvania Dutch way of life. Thousands of visitors enjoy traditional food, music, and crafts during this nine-day event.

Mummers Parade

A Quaker Colony

William Penn founding the colony of Pennsylvania

William Penn wanted Pennsylvania to be a place where people were free to pray any way they chose. His laws for the colony emphasized fairness and peace. He named the capital city Philadelphia, which means "City of Brotherly Love." Penn's ideas for Pennsylvania reflected the beliefs of his Quaker faith.

Did you know?
Quakers do not attend services in a church or temple. They go to meeting houses where they sit together and pray in silence.

Quaker meeting house

Quakers are members of a group called the Religious Society of Friends. They believe in freedom of religion and equal treatment for everyone. Penn's ideas about freedom and justice inspired parts of the Declaration of Independence and U.S. **Constitution**. Pennsylvania Quakers helped make the United States a country that values freedom for all.

Fast Facts About Pennsylvania

Pennsylvania's Flag

Pennsylvania's flag has a deep blue background. In the center are two horses holding up a coat of arms. The coat of arms shows a ship, a plow, and three bunches of wheat. A bald eagle sits atop the coat of arms. Beneath it is an olive branch and cornstalk wreath. A draped red ribbon holds the words of the state motto.

State Flower
mountain laurel

State Nicknames:	The Keystone State The Quaker State
State Motto:	"Virtue, Liberty, and Independence"
Year of Statehood:	1787
Capital City:	Harrisburg
Other Major Cities:	Philadelphia, Pittsburgh, Allentown
Population:	12,702,379 (2010)
Area:	46,055 square miles (119,282 square kilometers); Pennsylvania is the 33rd largest state.
Major Industries:	mining, manufacturing, farming, services
Natural Resources:	coal, natural gas, limestone, lumber, farmland
State Government:	203 representatives; 50 senators
Federal Government:	18 representatives; 2 senators
Electoral Votes:	20

State Bird
ruffed grouse

State Animal
white-tailed deer

Glossary

bluffs—cliffs or steep banks

Civil War—a war between the northern (Union) and southern (Confederate) states that lasted from 1861 to 1865

colonial—built by settlers from another country

colony—a territory owned and settled by people from another country

constitution—the basic laws and principles of a nation

diversity—variety of cultures or backgrounds

ethnic—from another country or cultural background

fertile—able to support growth

gorge—a deep, narrow valley with steep, rocky sides

Great Lakes—five large freshwater lakes on the border between the United States and Canada

mummers—actors or performers in costume

native—originally from a specific place

oil refineries—places where oil is turned into other products, such as gasoline

Pennsylvania Dutch—a group of people who came to Pennsylvania from Germany and Switzerland in the 1600s and 1700s; *Dutch* comes from the German word *Deutsch*, which means "German."

polka—a lively form of dance originally from Central Europe; polka is a dance for couples.

Quaker—a member of the Religious Society of Friends, a Christian faith known for its strong belief in peace

reenact—to perform a historical event

Revolutionary War—the war between 1775 and 1783 in which the United States fought for independence from Great Britain

scenic—providing beautiful views of the natural surroundings

service jobs—jobs that perform tasks for people or businesses

To Learn More

AT THE LIBRARY

Calkhoven, Laurie. *Will at the Battle of Gettysburg, 1863*. New York, N.Y.: Dutton Children's Books, 2011.

Figley, Marty Rhodes. *Who Was William Penn?: And Other Questions About the Founding of Pennsylvania*. Minneapolis, Minn.: Lerner, 2012.

Hart, Joyce, and Richard Hantula. *Pennsylvania*. New York, N.Y.: Marshall Cavendish Benchmark, 2011.

ON THE WEB

Learning more about Pennsylvania is as easy as 1, 2, 3.

1. Go to www.factsurfer.com.

2. Enter "Pennsylvania" into the search box.

3. Click the "Surf" button and you will see a list of related Web sites.

With factsurfer.com, finding more information is just a click away.

Index